The Life of

Samuel Pepys

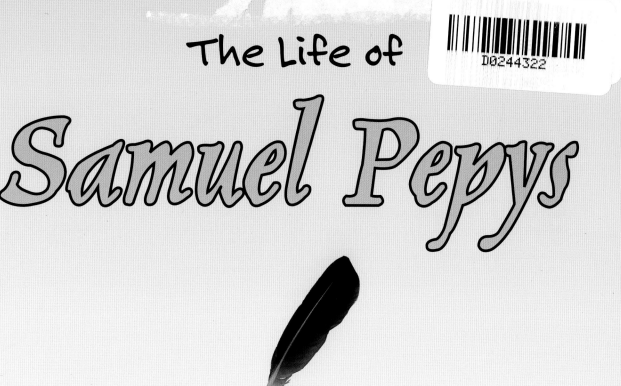

Emma Lynch

www.heinemann.co.uk/library

Visit our website to find out more information about **Heinemann Library** books.

To order:

Phone 44 (0) 1865 888066

Send a fax to 44 (0) 1865 314091

Visit the Heinemann Bookshop at www.heinemann.co.uk/library to browse our catalogue and order online.

First published in Great Britain by Heinemann Library, Halley Court, Jordan Hill, Oxford OX2 8EJ, part of Harcourt Education.
Heinemann is a registered trademark of Harcourt Education Ltd.

Editorial: Lucy Thunder and Harriet Milles
Design: Richard Parker and
    Tinstar Design Ltd (www.tinstar.co.uk)
Illustrations: Sam Thompson (Eikon Illustration)
Picture Research: Melissa Allison and Fiona Orbell
Production: Camilla Smith

Originated by Repro Multi-Warna
Printed and bound in China by
    South China Printing Company

The paper used to print this book comes from sustainable resources.

ISBN 978 0 431 18104 2 (hardback)
09 08 07 06 05
10 9 8 7 6 5 4 3 2 1

ISBN 978 0 431 18169 1 (paperback)
10 09
10 9 8 7 6 5 4 3 2

British Library Cataloguing in Publication Data
Emma Lynch
Samuel Pepys. – (The Life of)
942'.066'092
A full catalogue record for this book is available from the British Library.

Acknowledgements
The Publishers would like to thank the following for permission to reproduce photographs:
pp. **4, 9, 21** National Portrait Gallery; pp. **5, 6, 8** Mary Evans Picture Library; p. **9** Corbis/Edifice; p. **11** The Wellcome Trust Medical Photographic Library; pp. **12, 14, 19, 20, 24** The Pepys Library, Magdalene College, Cambridge; p. **13** Getty Images/Photodisc; p. **15** Bridgeman Art Library/Private Collection; p. **16** Bridgeman Art Library/Guildhall Library; pp. **17, 18** Topham Picturepoint; p. **22** Bridgeman Art Library/The House of Commons in Session, 1710 (oil on canvas), Tilemans, Peter (1684–1734)/Houses of Parliament, Westminster, London, UK; p. **23** Bridgeman Art Library/John Bethell; p. **25** TopFoto/UPPA Ltd.; p. **27** Duncan Grey; p. **26** The National Archives

Cover photograph of Samuel Pepys, reproduced with permission of Topham Picturepoint.
Page icons: Getty Images/Photodisc.

Every effort has been made to contact copyright holders of any material reproduced in this book. Any omissions will be rectified in subsequent printings if notice is given to the Publishers.

Contents

Words shown in the text in bold, **like this**, are explained in the Glossary.

Who was Samuel Pepys?

Samuel Pepys lived over 300 years ago. He wrote a famous **diary**. He wrote about his own life, and what life was like in London in the 1660s.

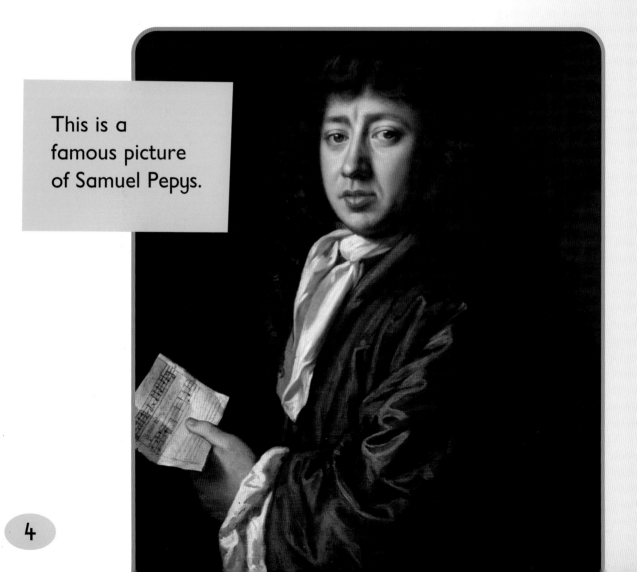

This is a famous picture of Samuel Pepys.

Samuel wrote about important events, such as the **Great Plague** and Great Fire of London. He also worked in the **government**.

London was much smaller when Samuel lived there than it is today.

Growing up in London

Samuel Pepys was born in London on 23 February 1633. He had five brothers and five sisters. Samuel's father made clothes. The family lived above his shop.

Samuel was born near Fleet Street in London.

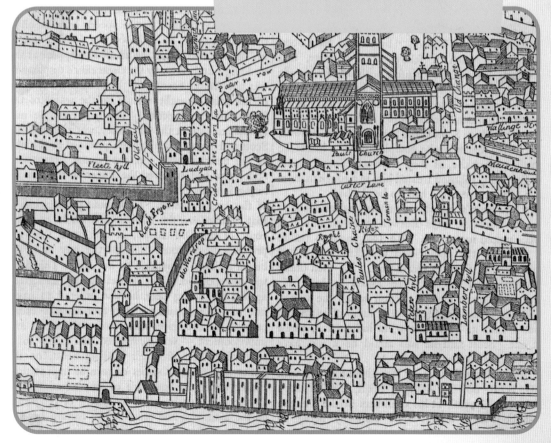

It was hard to stay clean in London at that time.

London was very dirty and full of chimney smoke. All the houses used wood fires for cooking and for keeping people warm.

A clever boy

Samuel was a clever boy. At St Paul's School, he learnt **Latin** and how to give speeches. Samuel loved books. He wanted to collect them when he grew up.

When Samuel left St Paul's School, he gave some books to the library.

Samuel went to Magdalene College. The college is part of Cambridge University.

In 1651, Samuel went to study at Cambridge University. While he was there he also learnt **shorthand** writing. This helped him to write quickly.

Samuel marries

In 1655, Samuel married Elizabeth de St Michel. She was only 15 years old. Samuel was 22 years old. Soon after his marriage, Samuel became very ill.

This is a picture of Elizabeth. In those days, girls often married when they were very young.

At that time, it was very dangerous and painful to have an **operation**. In March 1658, Samuel had a **kidney stone** removed. He felt much better afterwards.

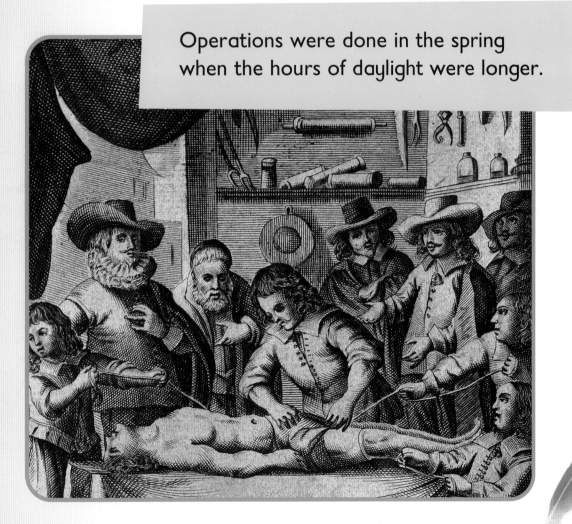

Operations were done in the spring when the hours of daylight were longer.

Writing a diary

Samuel began to work for the **navy** and King Charles II. He had to learn to make codes called **ciphers**. These were used to keep information secret.

Samuel used ciphers in his diary. He wanted to keep parts of it secret!

Samuel began to write a **diary** on 1 January 1660. He wrote in black or brown ink, with a **quill** pen. Samuel wrote every day, and used **shorthand**.

Quill pens were cut from feathers. Ink was kept in a pot.

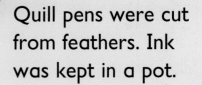

The Great Plague

In 1665, the **Great Plague** hit London. Many people became ill and died. Samuel and his wife left London. Samuel still visited the city to see what was happening.

Thousands of people died of the Great Plague.

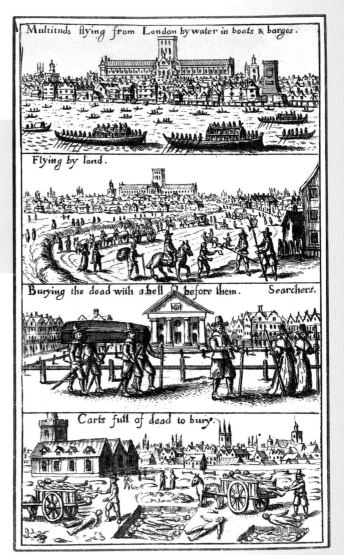

Samuel wrote about the Plague in his **diary**. He wrote 'It is feared that the number of dead this week is near 10,000.'

Samuel visited plague pits. People who died of the plague were buried there.

The Great Fire of London

When Samuel woke up on 2 September 1666, he saw a fire outside. He rushed to the top of the Tower of London. He wanted to see how far the fire had spread.

Samuel wrote in his **diary** of how he had 'seen the fire rage' and 'people running into boats'.

A fire engine, like this one, was used to put out the fire.

These Engins, (which are _____ the best) to quinch great Fires; are

JOHN KEELING Fecit

Samuel buried some of his belongings in his garden. He took some more to a friend's house, away from the fire. In the end, the fire did not reach Samuel's house.

Writing about his life

Samuel wrote about himself in his **diaries**. He even described what clothes he was wearing. He also wrote about his life at home with Elizabeth.

Samuel was very proud of being well dressed.

Samuel usually wrote in his diary at night.

Samuel wrote about the things he liked doing. He loved watching plays and spending time with friends. Often he would end a diary **entry** with the words 'And so to bed.'

End of the diary

Samuel had to read and write by candlelight. This hurt his eyes, and he was afraid he was going blind. He decided to stop writing his **diary**.

This is the last diary entry that Samuel ever wrote. Can you see the date?

Samuel wrote the last **entry** of his diary on 31 May 1669. He was 36 years old. Later that year, on 10 November, Samuel's wife died.

Elizabeth was only 29 years old when she died.

Samuel's last years

Samuel carried on working for many years. He worked for the **navy** and became a **Member of Parliament**. He collected books until he owned his own library.

Samuel often had to give speeches to Parliament about the navy.

Samuel became ill. He died in London on 26 May 1703, aged 70. He was buried next to his wife in St Olave's Church.

You can visit the graves of Samuel and Elizabeth in St Olave's Church in London.

Why is Samuel famous?

Samuel was an important writer. His **diaries** tell us about real life in London in the 1600s. He makes us feel as though we are there, too.

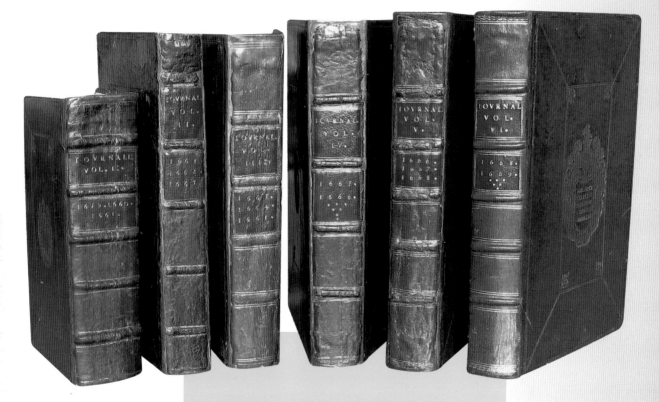

London in the 1600s comes to life in Samuel's diaries.

Samuel wrote very truthfully about himself and his own life. We learn a lot about the sort of man he was. He left all his books to Magdalene College, Cambridge.

This is the Samuel Pepys Library at Cambridge University.

More about Samuel

We can visit the Samuel Pepys Library in Cambridge. Here we can see his **diaries**. We can read his letters and see paintings of Samuel and Elizabeth.

Samuel wrote this letter to King James II.

We can visit the house at Brampton where Samuel lived as a young man.

We can also visit the **Museum** of London. Here you can see what London looked like when Samuel was alive. We can visit places that Samuel writes about in his diaries.

Fact file

- No-one was able to understand the code in Samuel's **diary** until 1819!

- The **Great Plague germs** came from fleas which lived on rats. The Plague ended in the winter, when the colder weather helped to kill off the fleas.

- The Great Fire started when a baker's shop caught fire in London. It lasted for four days.

- Between 1642 and 1649, there was a **Civil War** in England. Some people wanted the country to be led by a king. Others wanted the country to be led by **Parliament**. Parliament won the war. Samuel worked for Parliament until 1660, when King Charles II came back. Then Samuel worked for the king.

Timeline

1633   Samuel Pepys is born in London on 23 February

1651   Samuel goes to Magdalene College, Cambridge

1655   Samuel marries Elizabeth de St Michel

1660   Samuel writes the first entry of his diary on 1 January

1665   Samuel writes about the Great Plague in London

1666   Samuel writes about the Great Fire of London

1669   Samuel writes the last entry of his diary on 31 May

        Elizabeth Pepys dies on 10 November

1673–9   Samuel is MP for Castle Rising, Norfolk

1685   Charles II dies and James II becomes king

1703   Samuel dies on 26 May

Glossary

cipher code that keeps something you have written secret

Civil War war that happens when people from the same country fight against each other

diary daily record that someone writes about his or her own life

entry each time you write something in a diary

germs bacteria that make you ill

government group of people who run the country

Great Plague disease that killed thousands of people in London in 1665

kidney stone solid piece of material that can grow in the kidney

Latin language of Ancient Rome

Member of Parliament (MP) a person who is chosen to help run the country

museum place where important pieces of art or parts of history are kept for people to see

navy country's ships that are used in wars

operation something a doctor does to the body of a sick person to make them better

quill feather that is used as a pen

shorthand way of writing quickly

Find out more

Books

Firecat, Pippa Goodhat and Philip Hurst
(Egmont Books, 2002)

How do we know about…?: The Great Fire of London,
Deborah Fox (Heinemann Library, 2002)

How do we know about…?: The Great Plague,
Deborah Fox (Heinemann Library, 2002)

Samuel Pepys's Clerk, Philip Wooderson
(Franklin Watts, 2004)

Websites

www.pepys.info
Website with information about Samuel's life.

Places to visit

Museum of London, London Wall, London

Samuel Pepys Library, Magdalene College,
Cambridge

Index